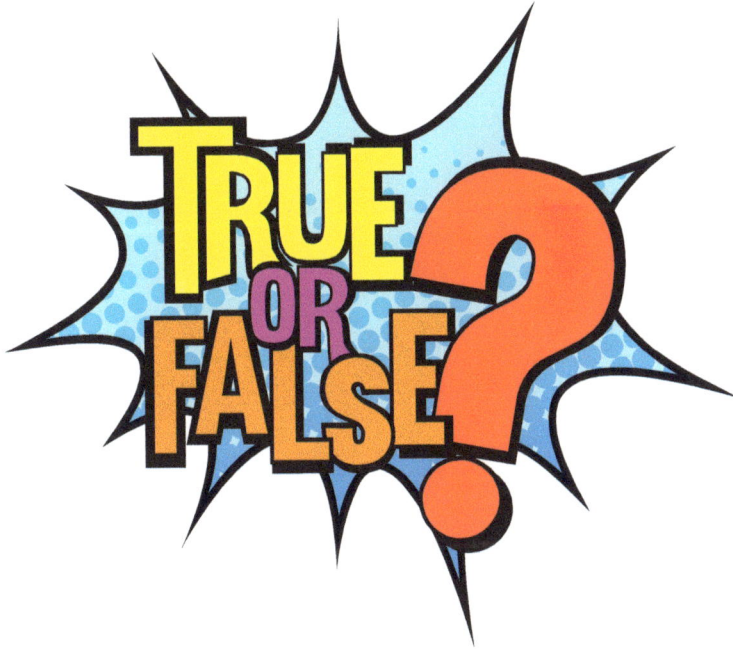

Co-published by agreement between Shi Tu Hui and World Book, Inc.

Shi Tu Hui
Room 1807, Block 1,
#3 West Dawang Road
Chaoyang District, Beijing 100025
P.R. China

World Book, Inc.
180 North LaSalle Street
Suite 900
Chicago, Illinois 60601
USA

Library of Congress Cataloging-in-Publication Data for this volume has been applied for.

True or False? (set #4)
ISBN: 978-0-7166-5417-9 (set, hc.)

Holidays and Celebrations
ISBN: 978-0-7166-5425-4 (hc.)

Also available as:
ISBN: 978-0-7166-5435-3 (e-book)
ISBN: 978-0-7166-5445-2 (soft cover)

Staff

Executive Committee

President
Geoff Broderick

Vice President, Editorial
Tom Evans

Vice President, Finance
Molly Stedron

Vice President, International and Marketing
Eddy Kisman

Vice President, Technology and Operations
Jason Dole

Director, Human Resources
Bev Ecker

Editorial

Writer
Lauren Kelliher

Manager, New Content
Jeff De La Rosa

Associate Manager, New Content
William D. Adams

Curriculum Designer
Caroline Davidson

Proofreader
Nathalie Strassheim

Graphics and Design

Coordinator, Design Development & Production:
Brenda Tropinski

Senior Visual Communications Designer
Melanie Bender

Senior Media Editor
Rosalia Bledsoe

Freelance Designer
Francis Lea

TRUE OR FALSE?

HOLIDAYS AND CELEBRATIONS

WORLD BOOK

www.worldbook.com

TRUE OR FALSE?

Holidays are celebrated all over the world.

TRUE!

Every country has its own special holidays. In Ireland, Saint Patrick's Day (March 17) is a legal holiday. In France, Joan of Arc's Day is celebrated the second Sunday of May. In Canada, National Indigenous Peoples Day is June 21.

TRUE OR FALSE?

A "bank holiday" is when banks give out free money.

FALSE!

A bank holiday is traditionally a day on which banks are closed. In the United States, President Franklin D. Roosevelt declared a bank holiday on March 6, 1933. He closed the banks to stop a money panic in the country. In Britain, *bank holiday* just means the same thing as *legal holiday*.

THE COMMERCIAL APPEAL

EXTRA   EXTRA

NATIONAL BANKING HOLIDAY IS ORDERED BY ROOSEVELT

President Takes Command of U.S. Supply of Gold

11

TRUE OR FALSE?

The most celebrated holiday in the United States is Valentine's Day.

FALSE!

Cupid strikes more than a few hearts. But, Christmas is probably the most celebrated holiday. Christians have celebrated the birth of Jesus Christ since the A.D. 300's. In time, both religious and nonreligious traditions developed around the holiday.

TRUE OR FALSE?

One of the biggest festivals in the world is a carnival.

TRUE!

Many carnivals developed from traditional festivals in Europe and grew to include elements of many cultures. The largest— Carnival—is held in Rio de Janeiro, Brazil, with samba dancing, balls, and parades.

TRUE OR FALSE?

All holidays began as religious feast days.

FALSE!

Many holidays have their roots in religious practices. But others celebrate *secular* (nonreligious) events, people, and causes. For example, many countries celebrate an independence day or other holiday honoring their nation.

23

TRUE OR FALSE?

During the Islamic holy month of Ramadan, people fast from sunrise to sunset.

TRUE!

During Ramadan, faithful Muslims may not eat or drink from morning until night. The end of Ramadan is celebrated by a great festival called Īd al-Fitr.

TRUE OR FALSE?

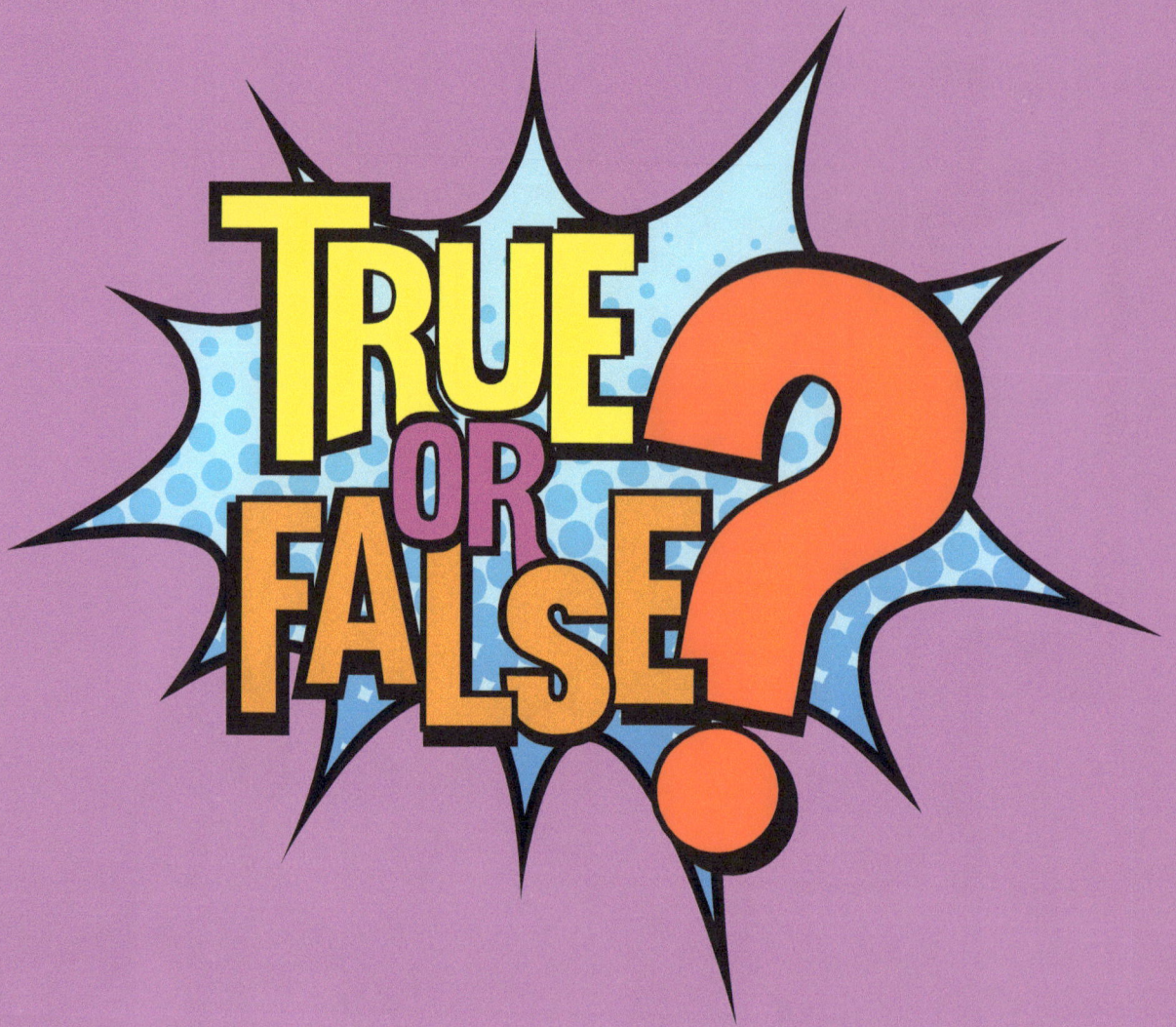

In Mexico, Día de los Muertos is a day when the dead are welcomed back to visit the living.

TRUE!

On Día de los Muertos, families create elaborate altars known as *ofrendas* (offerings) to welcome back the souls of departed family members and friends. They decorate the ofrendas with flowers, fruits, foods, sweets, and drinks.

TRUE OR FALSE?

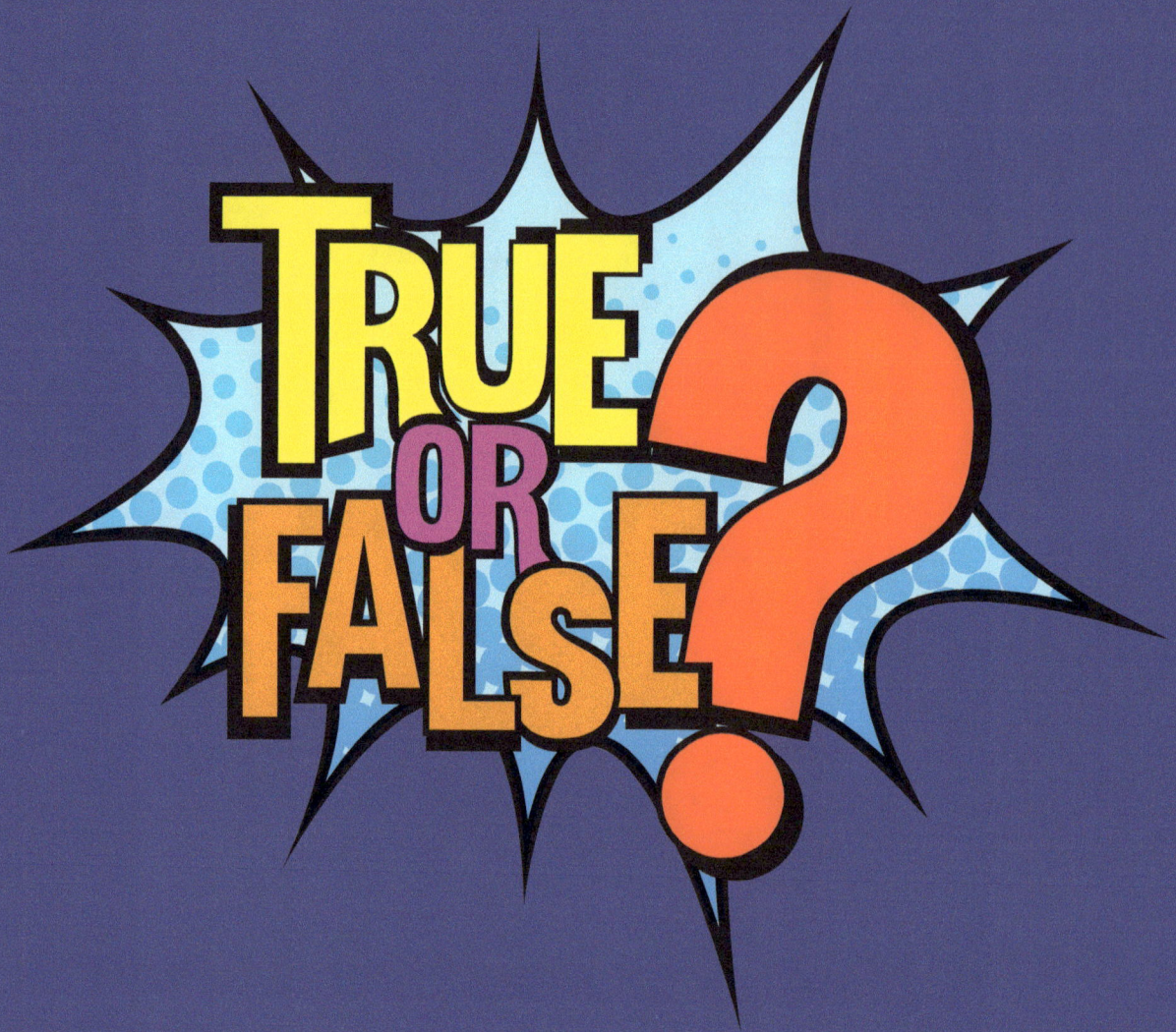

Some holidays have been celebrated
for thousands of years.

TRUE!

China's Qingming festival, or Tomb Sweeping Day, is 2,500 years old. On this day, people clean the graves of their ancestors to show respect. The festival started under the Zhou *dynasty* (family of rulers), which ruled from about 1045 to 256 B.C.

TRUE OR FALSE?

At the end of a harsh winter, Russian people celebrate by eating pancakes.

TRUE!

Maslenitsa is a Slavic religious and folk holiday also called Pancake Week. It is a week of games, parties, and of course, eating pancakes.

TRUE OR FALSE?

The Easter Bunny is based on the white rabbit from *Alice in Wonderland*.

FALSE!

Rabbits are associated with Easter and spring for their *fertility* (ability to produce many young). They don't have much to do with the Christian festival of Easter, which celebrates the resurrection of Jesus Christ.

TRUE OR FALSE?

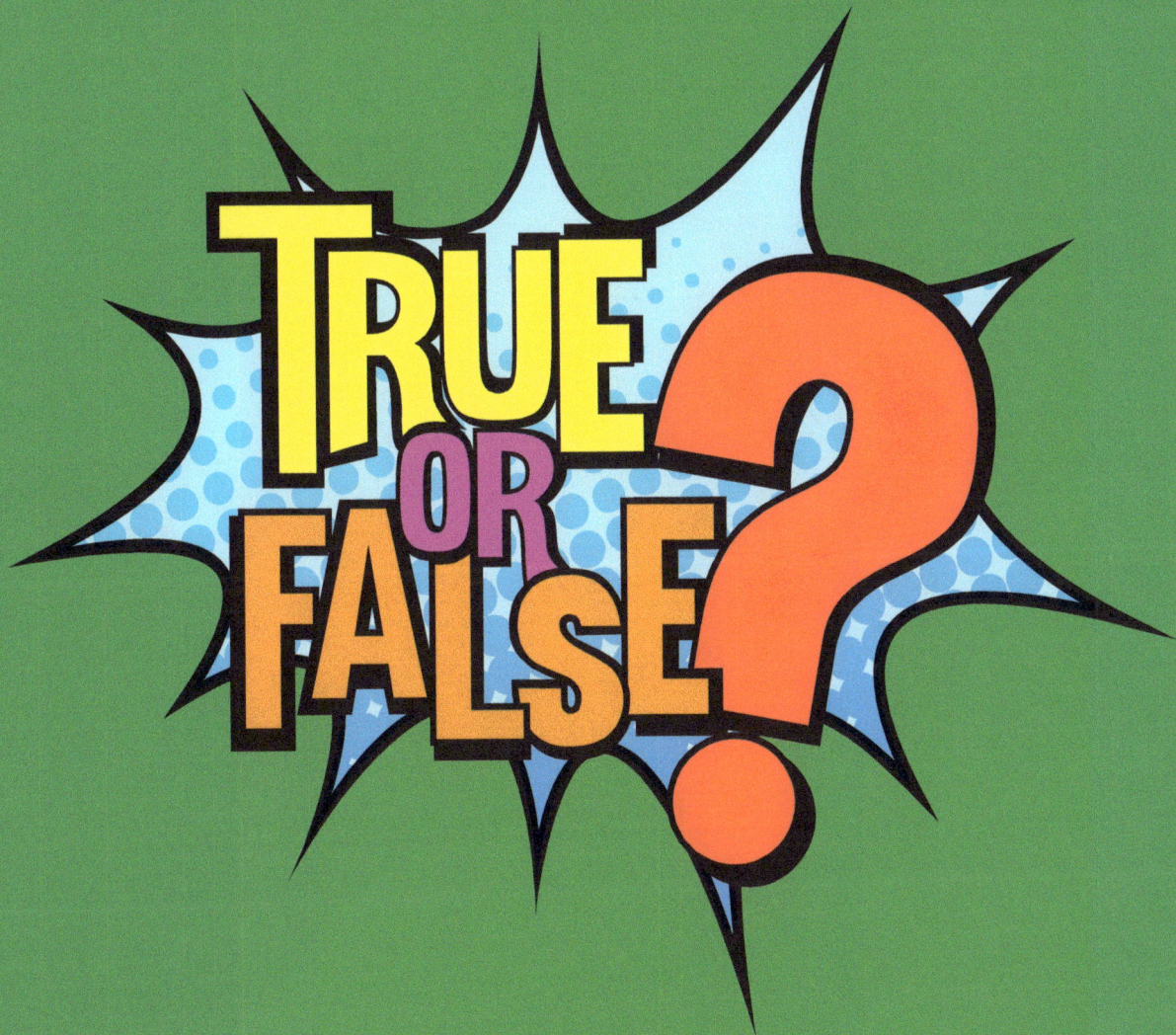

Jewish people celebrate a holiday known as the New Year of the Trees.

TRUE!

The Jewish holiday Tu b'shevat celebrates mother nature and all the earth has to offer. It is also called the New Year of the Trees.

TRUE OR FALSE?

Diwali, the festival of lights, honors the Hindu god Vishnu.

FALSE!

Diwali usually honors Lakshmi, the Hindu goddess of wealth. Holi, the festival of color, is associated with Vishnu, the god of preservation. On the eve of Holi, Hindus gather to sing and dance around giant bonfires that represent Vishnu's power.

TRUE OR FALSE?

Coming of Age Day is a Japanese holiday honoring those who turn 18.

FALSE!

In Japan, the public holiday Seijin Shiki, also called Adults Day, celebrates everyone who turns 20 years old. Ceremonies officially welcome youths into society as adults.

TRUE OR FALSE?

The first jack-o'-lanterns were carved from turnips, rather than pumpkins.

TRUE!

Jack-o'-lanterns are carved and displayed on Halloween to scare away spirits. The practice probably began with the carving of turnips in Ireland and Scotland.

01 JANUARY

TRUE OR FALSE?

Everyone celebrates the New Year on January 1st.

FALSE!

Many cultures celebrate the new year on a different day. New Year's celebrations include Rosh Ha-Shanah, also called Jewish New Year, and Lunar New Year, celebrated in China, Vietnam, and other Asian countries.

TRUE OR FALSE?

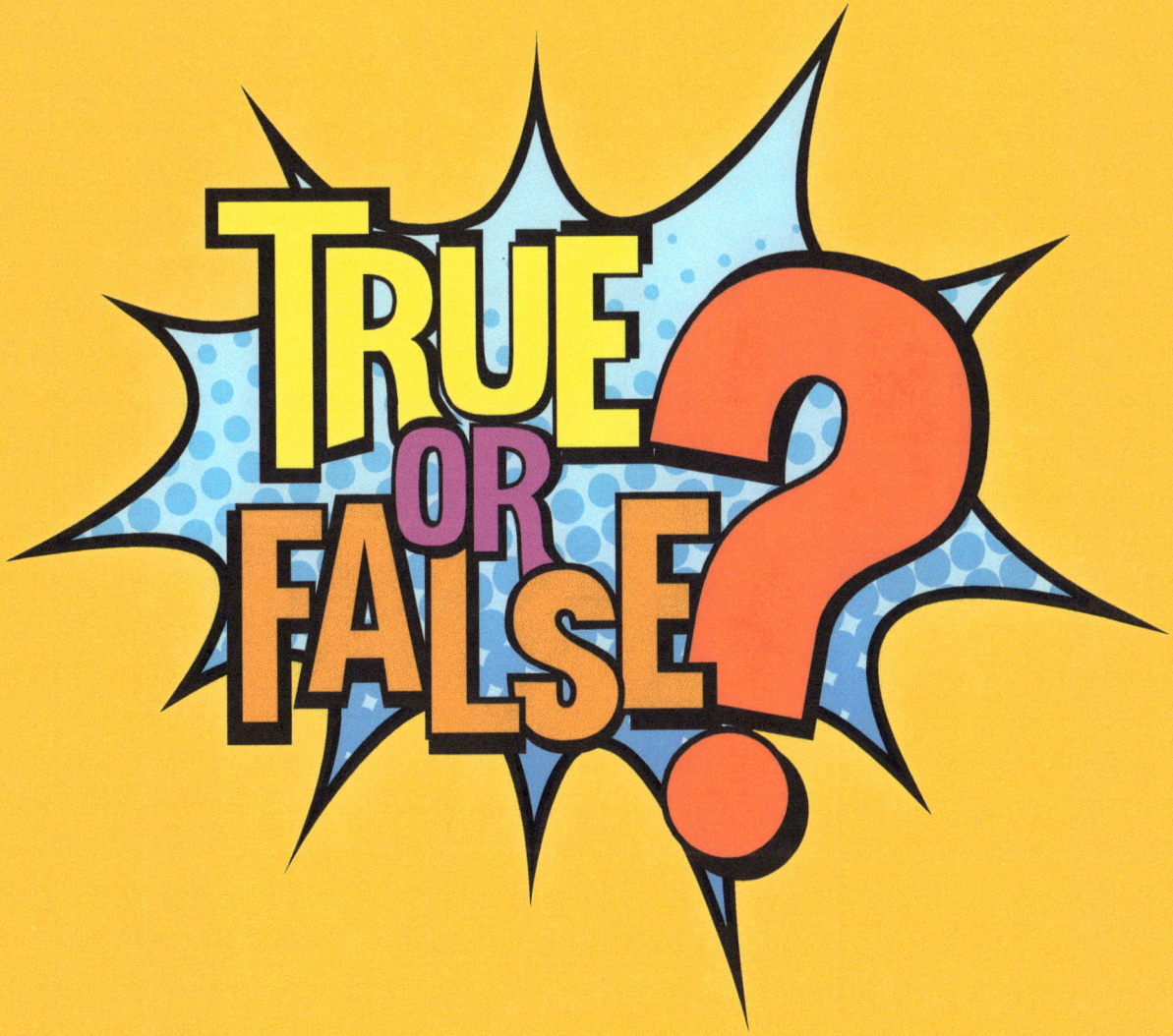

Up Helly Aa is Viking language for
"Lift up your torch!"

FALSE!

Up Helly Aa is a five-day Viking Festival in Lerwick, Shetland, Scotland. Started in the 1800's, the holiday celebrates Shetland's Viking history. Don't panic if you see folks dress up like the Vikings and set a traditional warship on fire in a special ceremony.

TRUE OR FALSE?

Elephants have a water fight every new year in Thailand.

TRUE!

Songkran, the Thai New Year, is celebrated with a water fight. The tradition began with the ritual of pouring water over statues of Buddha. The holiday has since evolved to include a giant water fight, complete with squirt guns and water-spouting elephants.

TRUE OR FALSE?

The festival La Tomatina has been called the world's biggest food fight.

TRUE!

La Tomatina is a tomato-throwing festival in the town of Buñol, near Valencia, Spain. Every year, about 20,000 people swarm the town center to throw 30,000 pounds (14,000 kilograms) of tomatoes at one another.

TRUE OR FALSE?

Saint Patrick is celebrated for finding the leprechaun's gold.

FALSE!

Saint Patrick was a missionary to Ireland in the A.D. 400's, converting the Irish to Christianity. In the United States, St. Patrick's Day is primarily a *secular* (nonreligious) celebration of Irish heritage.

TRUE OR FALSE?

Venetians throw a huge masquerade leading up to Mardi Gras.

TRUE!

In Italy, people celebrate the Carnival of Venice with decorated masks and ball gowns. The carnival ends on Shrove Tuesday, a Christian festival also known as Mardi Gras. Mardi Gras carnivals are celebrated in many cities around the world.

TRUE OR FALSE?

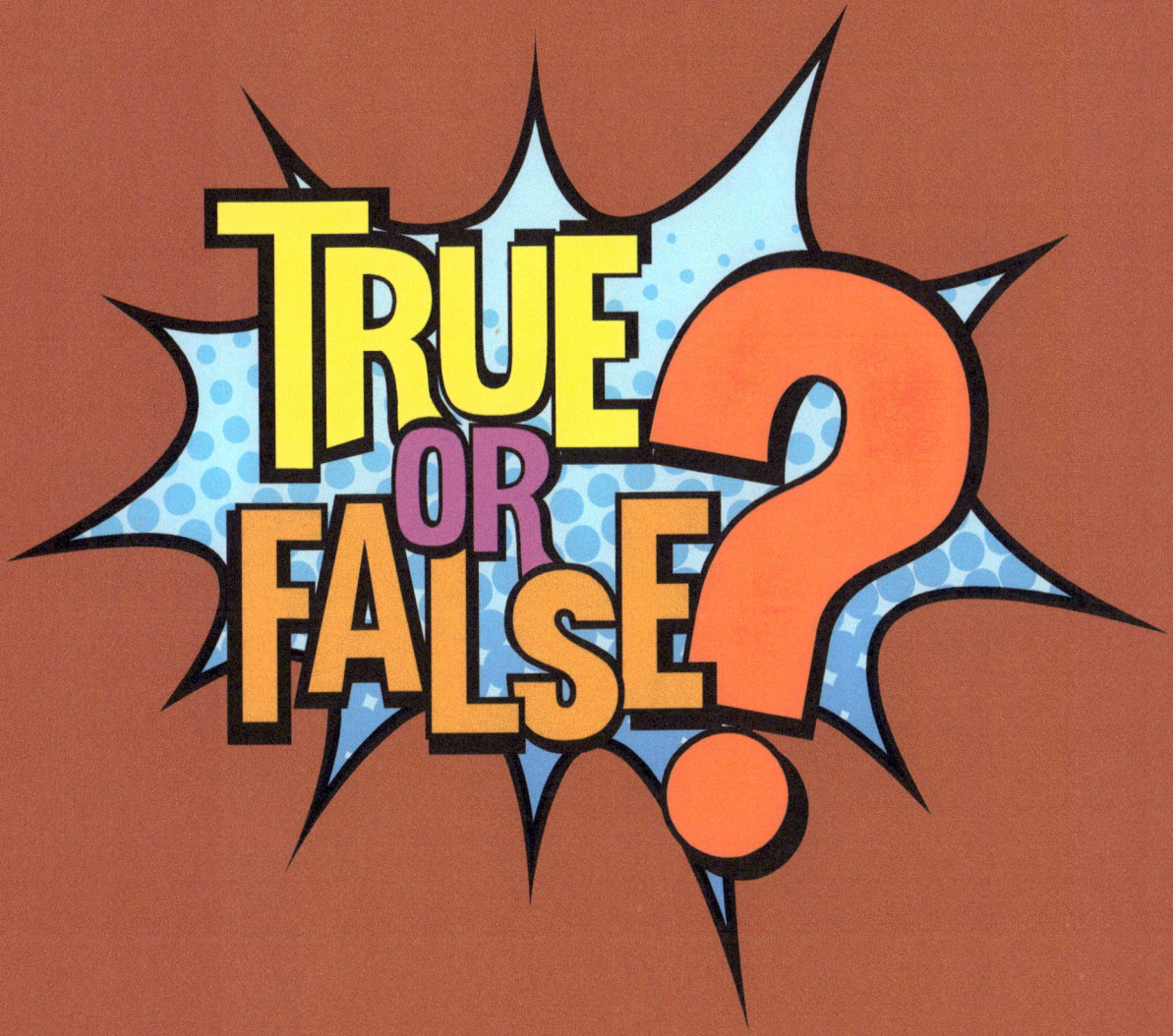

Boxing Day is an annual festive fight in the United Kingdom.

FALSE!

Boxing Day is the day after Christmas. The name may refer to boxes of gifts received by workers or to boxing up items for donation to the poor. (It doesn't refer to punching one another.)

TRUE OR FALSE?

Earth Day has been celebrated
for hundreds of years.

FALSE!

Earth Day is a relatively modern holiday. The first Earth Day observances were held April 22, 1970. People gathered to express care for the environment and concern for damage being done to it by human activities.

DID YOU KNOW...

**Colorful kites are
flown in Pakistan during the**
Basant Kite Flying Festival,
a Hindu festival celebrating spring.

The Burning Man festival
in Black Rock Desert, Nevada, gathers tens of
thousands of people each year for the biggest
open-air art exhibit in the world.

In honor of their patron saint, people celebrate **Saint David's Day** in Wales by wearing a daffodil.

Thailand's **Loy Krathong Festival** involves lighting lanterns and floating them to thank the water goddess.

Each race in the **Running of the Bulls,** part of the annual San Fermin Festival in Pamplona, Spain, lasts less than 4 minutes.

ENGAGE YOUR READER

GUIDED READING PROMPTS

Before Reading
- Allow readers to scan the text and discuss what they notice so far. Highlight the structure of this text and explain that the answers include both evidence and reasoning that support the claim of true or false.
- Explain the literacy skill: *Sometimes authors write a claim and then use evidence and reasoning to help make their point clear. Look for these elements as you read!*

During Reading
- Read each statement and provide time to discuss whether readers believe it to be true or false before turning the page to learn the facts.
- As you read, model how to identify the claims, evidence, and reasoning in the text. Prompt your readers to identify these features as they explore the text, too.
- Encourage readers to further discuss their learning by pausing to discuss surprising information.

After Reading
- Prompt your readers to connect, extend, and challenge their thinking about the text:
  - What will you take away from reading this text?
  - What changes in your thinking happened while reading and learning?
  - What is still challenging your thinking? What questions or wonderings do you still have?

LOOK BACK!
- Prompt readers to look back through the text to identify examples of interesting or thought-provoking claims.
- Challenge readers to explain what makes these examples so engaging.

CURRICULUM CONNECTIONS
These questions and tasks support the following English/Language Arts skills:
- Determining what a text says both explicitly and implicitly
- Citing specific evidence when drawing conclusions
- Interpreting words and phrases used in a text
- Analyzing how the structure of a text affects how it is read.

LITERACY SKILL

Authors make their claims stronger by supporting them with evidence and reasoning.

- A claim is a statement of truth.
- Evidence includes the facts or information that prove whether the claim is true.
- Reasoning includes any logical explanation that describes how the evidence supports the claim.

Examples from the text: Pages 68-71

- Claim: Elephants have a water fight every new year in Thailand.
- Evidence: People celebrate Songkran, the new year, with a giant water fight! Some bring squirt guns and buckets, others bring elephants.
- Reasoning: The tradition evolved from an older ritual where people would pour water over statues of Buddha.

EXTEND THROUGH WRITING

Challenge readers to create their own True/False questions and answers about holidays and celebrations.

- Have readers use a trusted reference, such as www.worldbookonline.com, to research information related to holidays and celebrations. Encourage readers to look for key details, fun facts, or surprising features that would make strong True or False statements.
- Give readers one notecard for each claim they research.
- Direct readers to write the claim on the front of the notecard. On the back, readers should describe why that claim is true or false using evidence and reasoning from their research.

MORE WAYS TO ENGAGE!

- Play a game! After considering each claim, have readers signify "true" with a thumb up and "false" with a thumb down. Keep score to see who knows their facts about holidays and celebrations the best!
  - Develop collaboration skills by grouping readers together into teams.
- Further discuss any True/False claims that revealed readers' misconceptions. Focus the conversation on *why* they initially thought what they did and how the text helped them learn.

Acknowledgments

Cover © Ground Picture/Shutterstock;
© Kolonko/Shutterstock; © Fad82/
Shutterstock;
© Kotoffei/Shutterstock

6-9 © Shutterstock
10-11 Library of Congress; Public Domain
12-31 © Shutterstock
32-33 © CPA Media Pte/Alamy Images
34-35 © Imaginechina Limited/Alamy Images
36-39 © Ira Lichi, Shutterstock
40-41 © AF Fotografie/Alamy Images
42-73 © Shutterstock
74-75 © Steve Davey Photography/Alamy
Images
76-77 © ADragan/Shutterstock
78-79 © ADragan/Shutterstock; © Chronicle/
Alamy Images
80-91 © Shutterstock
92-93 © Lukas Bischoff, Alamy Images;
© benemale/Shutterstock; © Darya
Petrenko, Alamy Images; © Migel/
Shutterstock; © Yanushevskaya Victoria,
Shutterstock
96 © Sudowoodo/Shutterstock